COMPOUND THINKING

How I used AI to protect my people,

preserve our voice,

and get time back

Sam Shavers

Communications Architect · Black Technologist

Chester, Pennsylvania

COMPOUND THINKING

How I used AI to protect my people, preserve our voice, and get time back

© 2025 Sam Shavers. All rights reserved.

No part of this book may be reproduced, stored in a retrieval system, or transmitted in any form or by any means — electronic, mechanical, photocopying, recording, or otherwise — without prior written permission from the author, except for brief quotations in critical articles, reviews, teaching, ministry, or community training contexts.

Printed in the United States.

ISBN (paperback): 9798274308137

Cover design: [Sam Shavers / Kingdom Communications]
Photography / Concept Art: Kitchen Table Series

First Edition

DEDICATION

For everyone who ever called me and said,
"Can you help me with this real quick?"

You are the reason this exists.

TABLE OF CONTENTS

Foreword ... i

Introduction: Why This Book Exists ... 1

Chapter 1. The Chester Table ... 9

Chapter 2. The Break Point ... 17

Chapter 3. Compound Thinking ... 27

Chapter 4. The Church Broadcast Room ... 37

Chapter 5. Funerals, Memory, Dignity ... 47

Chapter 6. Teaching the Kids ... 59

Chapter 7. Teaching the Elders ... 69

Chapter 8. Politics, Messaging, Winning ... 79

Chapter 9. CAAT, Tara, and the Future ... 89

Chapter 10. What You Do Next ... 99

Resources ... 111

Notes ... 113

Acknowledgments ... 115

About the Author ... 117

FOREWORD

by Tara Jones, Founder & CEO, Chester Cultural Arts and Technology Center (CAAT)

Sam has asked me to write the foreword to his book Compound Thinking, and honestly, there's no greater honor than speaking about someone whose work I've seen not just succeed but serve.

I've known Sam for years. We grew up in the same city, shared the same sense of responsibility to our community, and often found ourselves showing up to solve the same problems, sometimes with no budget, no rest, and no blueprint, just heart and purpose. What always struck me about Sam wasn't just his technical skill. It was his ability to see through the noise and find the human center in every story, every livestream, every broadcast, every family he helped.

One time, I remember walking into church one Sunday and seeing Sam working with teenagers, cables, and cameras, all working like an orchestra. He wasn't just "running media." He was building a bridge between generations. He was showing young people that technology wasn't just for Silicon Valley; it was for Chester, too. He was proving that our stories were worth telling with the same quality and dignity as anyone else's.

That's the spirit of Compound Thinking. This isn't a theory or a trend. It's a lived experience, a system born out of exhaustion, compassion, and the determination to protect what matters most: people, culture, and time. Sam turned a kitchen table into a control room, a classroom, and a think tank. Through it, he built something bigger than content; he built capacity.

In these pages, Sam invites you into that process. He doesn't just talk about using AI; he shows how it can give us time back, time to rest, to teach, to lead, to think. This book is a roadmap for anyone who carries too much, cares too deeply, and keeps showing up anyway.

If you've ever been "the one everyone calls," Compound Thinking will feel like home and like hope.

Tara Jones
Founder & CEO, Chester Cultural Arts and Technology Center

INTRODUCTION

WHY THIS BOOK EXISTS

I didn't sit down to write a book because I had free time.

I sat down because I hit a wall.

For years, I was the one people called when anything needed to be captured, streamed, fixed, designed, recorded, or put out to the world with dignity.

If a church needed to go live on Sunday? Call Sam.
If a young person wanted to learn how to film? Call Sam.
If an older auntie couldn't figure out her phone and felt embarrassed? Call Sam.
If somebody's loved one passed and the family needed a funeral program, slideshow, livestream, obituary words, all done by morning? Call Sam.
If a local politician needed clean messaging to reach people who've stopped believing in politics? Call Sam.

That sounds like respect on paper. In real life it was pressure.

I wasn't sleeping. I wasn't eating right. I wasn't thinking about myself. I was operating like an emergency line for a whole city.

Then I caught COVID.

That moment changed my life.

I went from moving non-stop to being stuck in place. I was in my space, alone, sick, and I couldn't run out and fix everything for everybody. I couldn't "just do it" with my hands like I always did. I had to sit.

And while I was sitting, I found AI.

This was early — before most people had even touched it, before the hype cycle, before your cousin started posting "I made a logo in 3 seconds." I'm talking about before it was public. I started feeding it problems. And it started giving me back pieces of my time.

That's when I knew the world was about to change.

That's when I knew my world had to change.

Not because AI is magic. But because I saw instantly that if I trained it the right way, it could sit next to me and take some of the weight.

I realized something I had never had before: time to think.

Understand what that means. When I say "think," I don't mean daydream. I mean thinking at the systems level, not at the task level.

Before:
I was always in task mode. Cut this clip. Export this reel. Make this funeral program by morning. Clean this candidate's caption so it lands without blowing up. Fix this audio before Bible study starts. Answer the grandmother. Calm the family. Rewrite the post so it hits the right group.

After:
I saw that I could make machines handle repetitive, mechanical, pixel-level jobs — so I could pull up and build pipelines. I could start solving root problems, not just putting out smoke.

That shift is the birth of what I call Compound Thinking.

This book is the story of how I used AI to build systems that protect my people.

It's not "how to get rich with AI."
It's not "10 prompts to optimize your hustle."
It's not theory.

This is field notes from Chester, Pennsylvania:
– Church broadcast rooms.
– Old heads and aunties trying to FaceTime their grandkids.
– Grieving families who deserve honor, not chaos and cheap flyers.
– After-school kids with phones who don't know they're already holding a production studio.
– City leadership that needs real messaging to actually win and then serve.
– A neighborhood culture that's bigger than the news ever shows.

I'm writing this so somebody else doing this work — in a different city, different block, different ministry, different family — can stop breaking their own body trying to hold everybody together.

If you are the person everyone calls when something goes wrong, this is for you.

This is Compound Thinking.

CHAPTER 1

THE CHESTER TABLE

Most of this book was built at a beat-up wooden table.

Not a boardroom.
Not a lab.
Not a clean coworking space.
My kitchen table.

The surface is scratched and scarred from years of real life. Cables everywhere. A laptop with waveforms up. An iPad. A Styrofoam cup because I've been here for hours. Printed funeral programs next to handwritten run sheets. A list of who's reading scripture, in what order, with what mic. A post-it with someone's aunt's name spelled right, because getting that name wrong would wound the whole family.

And also: my phone blowing up.

"You live-streaming tonight?"
"Can you send that clip to me?"
"Can you fix this audio?"
"My mom needs help getting back into her Facebook."
"Can you teach my son how to do video like you?"
"We're gonna need the service. Can you do the service?"

That table became a command center. But not for a company.
For a community.

When people talk about "tech," they talk about apps, scale, market. What I'm running is none of that.
I'm running care.

At this table, I am:
– Producer
– Editor
– Broadcast engineer
– Political comms
– Grief support
– Youth mentor
– Tech support for elders
– Archivist
– Family historian
– Crisis PR
– And sometimes the only one picking up the phone at 2 a.m.

Each of those roles on its own could be a full-time job. I was doing all of them at once.

This is where Compound Thinking starts: not in theory, but right here at the table. Real equipment, real names, real funerals, real kids, real church, real politics, real city.

CHAPTER 2

THE BREAK POINT

Before COVID, I was already worn down.

I helped run Balanced Communications Group with Teresa and Jenn. We were trying to be a remote, post-pandemic communications shop before that was normal.

We had skill. But keeping creatives paid, keeping clients happy, doing the travel, getting the shots, editing deliverables — it was constant fire.

Then we hit the part no one talks about: you build the machine, but the machine runs on you.

If somebody doesn't follow through, guess who has to fix it.
If you're the reliable one, guess who ends up doing five people's work.

We learned hard lessons. We were moving like a real shop, but it was costing us.

Then Teresa passed.

Losing her wasn't just losing a teammate. It was losing a piece of belief. It made it clear how fragile this all was. We talked about streamlining. We talked about automation. We talked about "How do we not get stuck holding all of this forever?"

But we were still basically doing it by hand.

Then I got sick.

COVID pinned me down. I wasn't out filming. I wasn't running cords through a church balcony. I wasn't chasing three different clients across two different cities.

I was stuck in my own space for real, for the first time in a long time.

And this is when I met AI.

Before it was public, I was already in it.

I remember thinking:
This thing is going to change everything.
This is going to let me stop doing every little step by hand.
This is going to let me think.

Not just make content faster. Think.

That's when the mindset changed. I stopped seeing myself as the guy who "does content," and I started seeing myself as infrastructure.

CHAPTER 3

COMPOUND THINKING

Compound Thinking = letting your work stack instead of reset.

In the old way:
– Every project is brand new.
– Every crisis is brand new.
– Every livestream is a fresh fire drill.
– Every funeral program starts from a blank file at 1:17 a.m.

In Compound Thinking:
– The setup you built for one Sunday broadcast becomes a template you re-use for the next five.
– The caption style you wrote for that councilman campaign becomes a messaging guide for the next person who steps up.
– The funeral layout you made for one grieving family becomes a respectful, repeatable starting point so the next grieving family can breathe instead of panic.
– The social media kit you built for the church becomes a training handout for the kids so they can start running it themselves.

Before AI, I was doing that reuse manually, slowly, in my head.

After AI, that reuse became repeatable, documentable, teachable.

The work started compounding.

People will call that "scaling." I don't. I call it capacity.

Capacity is survival.
Capacity is "I don't die doing this."
Capacity is "I can teach the kid in the back row to switch cameras

during service, and he can do it next Sunday without me."
Capacity is "the auntie can go live on her phone and pin a comment and talk to her people without me driving across town first."
Capacity is "the city doesn't lose its memory every time one of our elders passes."

When you build capacity, you're not just helping. You're building infrastructure.

That's Compound Thinking.

CHAPTER 4

THE CHURCH BROADCAST ROOM

When people saw the livestream from the church, they saw a clean multi-camera feed, good audio, lower thirds, smooth switches. They saw quality. They saw "Who's running their media? That looks official."

What they didn't see:
– I'm in a side room with cables everywhere.
– I'm training teenagers live while the service is happening.
– I'm quietly fixing audio and graphics on the fly.
– I'm making sure the person at the podium is framed with respect.
– And while I'm doing that, my phone is buzzing for something completely unrelated that still matters.

Church wasn't just church. It was broadcast training school, youth mentorship, crisis communications, and historical archive all in one.

Here's how AI plugged in:

I started using AI to:
– generate first-pass captioning and sermon summaries,
– prep social cuts faster,
– document the run of show so next week didn't start from zero,
– lay out lower-thirds templates the kids could reuse instead of asking me for every graphic.

The point wasn't "AI replaced me."

The point was "AI made it so I didn't have to sit in that chair forever for this to survive."

Because if I get sick? If I burn out? If I move?

Does the message stop?

Now — it doesn't have to.

CHAPTER 5

FUNERALS, MEMORY, DIGNITY

This is the heaviest part of the work.

Someone passes.
The family is wrecked.
There's paperwork. There's pain. There's confusion. There's no sleep. There's sometimes drama. There's always heartbreak.

And on top of that:

"Who's doing the program?"
"Who's got a good picture of Grandma?"
"Can we get a slideshow?"
"Can we stream it for the cousins who can't make it?"

That moment is sacred. You cannot be sloppy with that.

I started building respectful, beautiful funeral programs and livestreams on short notice. Photo restoration. Slideshows. Music. Camera angles that don't feel invasive. Title cards with the right spelling, the right dates, the right honor.

Families will remember forever how you handled that service.

AI's role here wasn't "make it fake."

AI's role was:
"I'll draft the layout. I'll clean the background. I'll enhance the photo so she looks how she should be remembered. I'll pull the first pass of the obituary formatting so you're not starting at a blank screen at 2 a.m. while crying."

That's not automation.

That's mercy.

CHAPTER 6

TEACHING THE KIDS

The next piece was youth.

I'm in the church broadcast booth with teenagers. I'm at CAAT with kids after school. I'm literally sitting them in front of production gear and saying: "This isn't magic. You can do this. You can run this."

I also train them on phone media:
– how to frame a shot,
– how to stabilize,
– how to speak on camera,
– how to tell a story that's not just "look at me," but "this is what's happening in my city."

Here's where AI fits:

I use AI to give them instant transcripts, captions, story outlines, even basic social edits — not so they never learn editing, but so they can see themselves WIN fast.

When a kid goes from "I don't know how" to "I made this and people watched it," everything changes. Confidence. Literacy. Voice. Employment path.

That's not content.

That's a path out.

CHAPTER 7

TEACHING THE ELDERS

On the other end, I'm sitting with elders.

I'm showing them:
– how to unlock the phone,
– how to make a video call,
– how to hit "go live" without fear,
– how to not get scammed,
– how to talk to their grandbabies.

This is digital safety. Digital presence. Digital respect.

AI shows up here by making me faster at building instructions, screenshots, handouts, one-click explainers in plain language. I can generate a guide in that person's tone, not in cold "tech support" tone.

The seniors aren't behind.

They just weren't invited.

My job is to invite them.

CHAPTER 8

POLITICS, MESSAGING, WINNING

When I stepped in as Director of Communication for Councilman Fred Green in Chester, I applied the same mentality:

– Clean messaging.
– Fast turnaround.
– Same voice every time so people trust you.
– Visibility, not noise.

I automated large chunks of campaign communication: social posts, talking points, tone, rollout rhythm. Not to make it fake — to make it consistent.

That let him spend his energy on people instead of scrambling content.

He won.

That was proof: this system doesn't just make pretty videos. It moves outcomes.

CHAPTER 9

CAAT, TARA, AND THE FUTURE

The Chester Cultural Arts and Technology Center (CAAT) is where this becomes bigger than me.

Tara Jones — who I grew up with — is the CEO. Her vision and my vision line up: tech, culture, youth, legacy.

We're turning what I've been doing at the table into physical infrastructure:

– media labs,
– training rooms,
– spaces where kids and elders can sit in the same building and both be supported,
– a pathway where this kind of communications work becomes a job, not just a favor.

That's what Compound Thinking scales into:
not "how do I do more,"
but "how do WE carry this together."

I'm not trying to be the hero forever. I'm trying to build something that outlives me.

CHAPTER 10

WHAT YOU DO NEXT

This last chapter is for whoever's reading this and saying: "That's me. I'm the one everybody calls. How do I not fall apart?"

Step 1. Map your load.

Write down EVERY job you're doing for people. Be honest.

Step 2. Identify the work that MUST be human.

Comforting a grieving family? Human.
Advising a scared kid? Human.
Telling a grandmother she matters and she's allowed to be seen? Human.

Step 3. Push everything else off your plate.

Captioning, layout, cutting clips, stabilizing video, basic design, first draft messaging, calendar reminders, template documents — hand it to AI. Not because you're lazy. Because those are not the sacred parts.

Step 4. Turn repeat pain into a repeat system.

Any time you say "I'm doing this again," that is a pipeline waiting to be built.

Step 5. Teach somebody else how to run the pipeline.

That's how you stop being a single point of failure.

That's how you get time back.

That's Compound Thinking.

When you build capacity, you're not just helping.
You're building infrastructure.

I am not selling innovation.
I am documenting survival.

— Sam Shavers, Chester, PA

RESOURCES

Compound Thinking doesn't stop with this book.

Use this page as a starting point to build your own systems, not just copy mine. As my work grows, the tools, checklists, and examples will grow too.

For up-to-date resources connected to this book, look for:

– Digital workshops and trainings on Compound Thinking
– Templates for church media, funerals, campaigns, and community projects
– Sample workflows for youth and elder technology programs
– Behind-the-scenes breakdowns of real projects from Chester, PA

To find the latest material, search for "Compound Thinking by Sam Shavers" on your favorite platforms or visit the online links shared in my public talks, workshops, and social media. However you get to it, the goal is the same: protect your people, preserve your voice, and get your time back.

NOTES

Use this space to capture your own systems, ideas, and reminders.

What are the places in your world where everybody calls you first?

What can you hand to a machine, and what will always need your human touch?

This page is for you to start sketching your version of Compound Thinking.

ACKNOWLEDGMENTS

This work is never one person.

To my city, Chester, PA.
To my family.
To the elders who trusted me with their face and their voice.
To the kids who sat in that booth and took the controls.
To the families who let me help hold memory during the heaviest hours.
To the pastors and church leaders who said "Yes, let's go live."
To Councilman Fred Green.
To Tara Jones and CAAT for seeing this not as "content," but as infrastructure.
To Teresa Coble and Jenn Hartzell — Balanced Communications forever.
To everyone who ever said, "Sam, can you help real quick?"

This book is proof that I heard you.

ABOUT THE AUTHOR

Sam Shavers is a communications architect and Black technologist from Chester, Pennsylvania. He has spent his life behind the camera, in the livestream booth, at the kitchen table, and on the phone at all hours — documenting, translating, protecting, and amplifying.

He served as a Navy combat cameraman and mass communication specialist, traveling the world under pressure and capturing truth for commanders, sailors, media, and history. After returning home, he became the person everybody called — for livestreaming church, preserving elders' voices, training youth to create, building respectful homegoing media for grieving families, and helping local leaders win their message.

Sam's work is grounded in his "FOE" ethos — Family Over Everything — and in a commitment to make sure Black stories from cities like Chester are told with dignity, accuracy, and care. Through Compound Thinking, he uses AI not as a gimmick, but as a way to take the routine work off his body so he can protect his people, build capacity, and leave infrastructure behind for the next generation.

His work is about giving people their voice while they're still here, and preserving that voice with dignity when they're gone.

Made in the USA
Middletown, DE
05 December 2025